Incredible Action Origami

that really works

Paul Jackson

CONTENTS

Introduction 2

Read This! 2

Symbols 3

Twirly-Copter 4

Tumbler 6

Double-Vision 10

Waterbomb 12

Jumping Frog 16

Jaws 19

Propeller 22

Whip-Crack 24

Flapping Bird 28

LOWELL HOUSE JUVENILE

LOS ANGELES

Introduction

This book brings folded paper to life by showing you how to make incredible action origami designs that spin, tumble, jump, and flap!

There are many thousands of origami designs, but very few that can be played with, so the action designs in this book are not only fun, but also very special. They are all classics, old and new, collected from around the origami world.

Action origami only truly comes alive when you share your favorite designs with friends. But before you begin, please read Read This! below and look at the Symbols page opposite. Together, they will tell you all you need to know to make your paper come to life.

 # Read This!

Here are some important tips to make your action origami work well.

- **_Find a Good Place to Work._** Fold the paper on a hard, flat surface so that you can press every crease firmly.

- **_Ask an Adult._** When you are using scissors, ask an adult to supervise.

- **_Follow the Steps Carefully._** When making an action origami design, keep checking to make sure that it looks exactly like the step-by-step drawings. If it doesn't ... don't panic! Just go back one or two steps until what you are making looks like the earlier drawing, then try again. Also, don't just look at the drawings —read the instructions, too!

- **_Work Slowly. Don't Rush!_** All the action origami designs in the book will work better and look better if you make them slowly and carefully. Sometimes you may need to make a design two or three times before you can make it really well.

- **_Good Paper._** Fold the designs using clean, uncrumpled paper. Notepaper or printer paper is best. Use 21.5 x 28 cm (8½ x 11in) paper.

Symbols

These simple symbols explain how to make the designs in the book. If you see a symbol in the instructions and you don't understand it, look back to this page to see what it means.

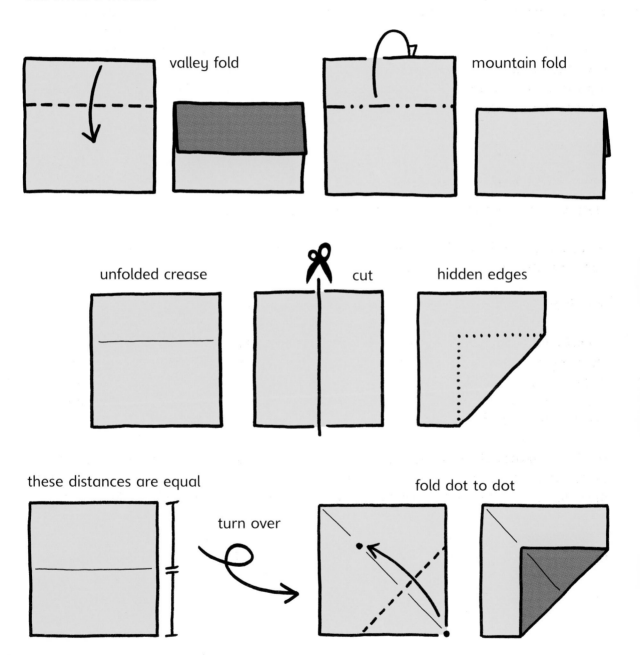

valley fold

mountain fold

unfolded crease

cut

hidden edges

these distances are equal

turn over

fold dot to dot

Twirly-Copter

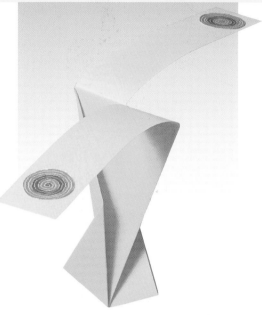

This design spins so fast that it takes an amazingly long time to reach the ground.

Use a 25 x 5cm (10 x 2in) strip of paper and scissors.

1

A — — — B

C — — D

2

C — D

A — B

3

C — D

B — A

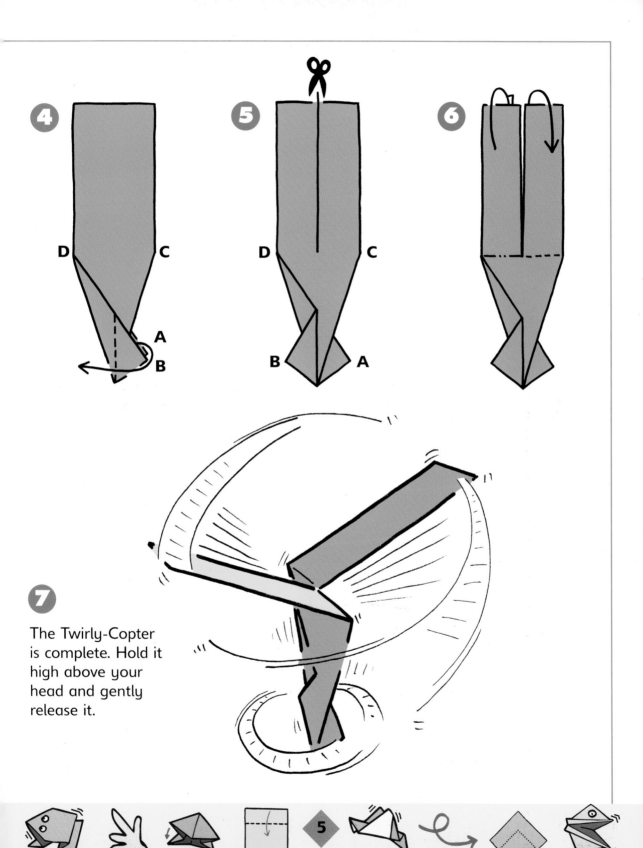

4

D   C

A
B

5

D   C

B   A

6

7

The Twirly-Copter is complete. Hold it high above your head and gently release it.

Tumbler

The top-heavy design of this fun toy is the secret to its long tumble. It is based on a famous toy by the Japanese origami master Seiryo Takekawa.

 Use 21.5 x 28cm (8½ x 11in) paper.

1 Fold in half lengthwise, crease, and unfold. Then fold a triangle and unfold.

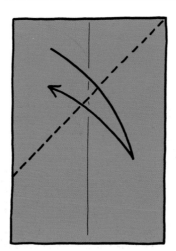

2 Fold dot to dot as shown.

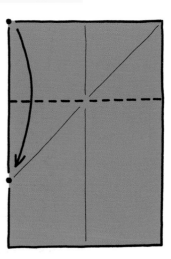

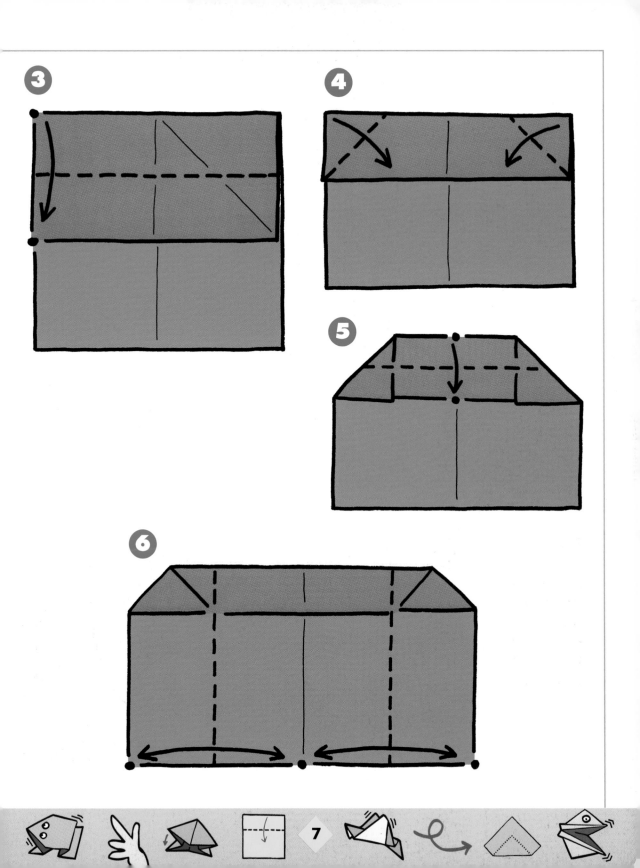

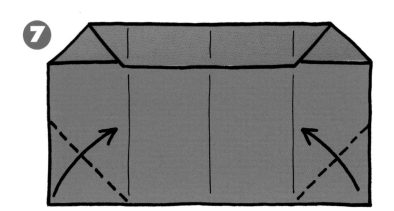

7

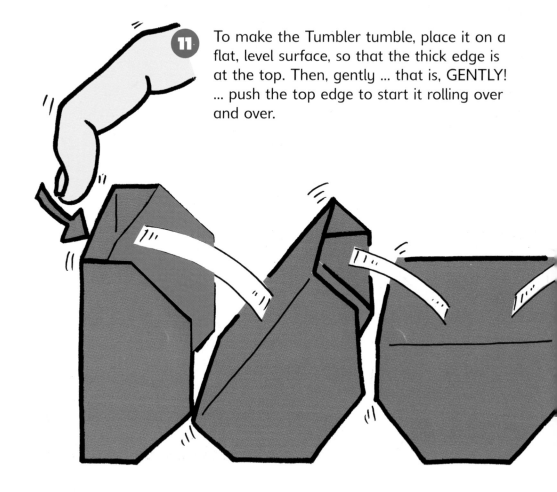

11 To make the Tumbler tumble, place it on a flat, level surface, so that the thick edge is at the top. Then, gently ... that is, GENTLY! ... push the top edge to start it rolling over and over.

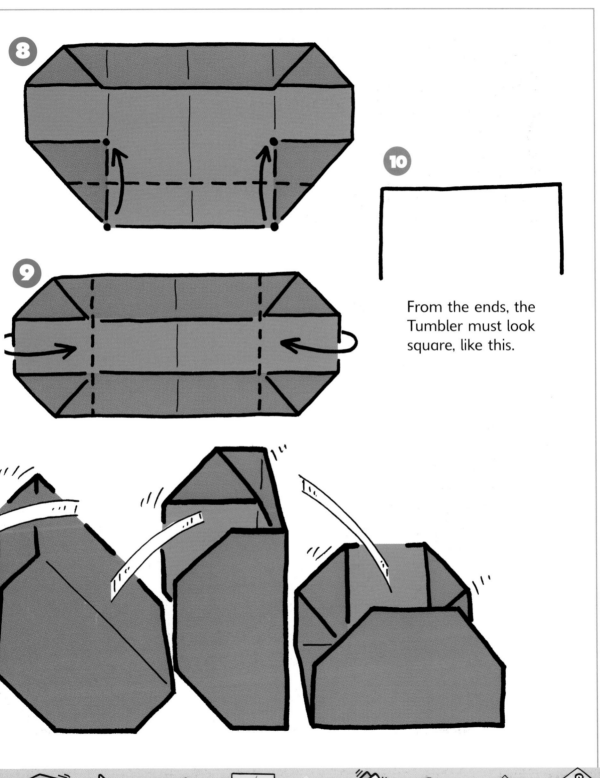

8

9

10

From the ends, the Tumbler must look square, like this.

Double-Vision

This clever illusion tricks the brain into thinking it sees one complete picture, when it actually sees two pictures, one after the other. The effect is known to science as the Retention of Vision.

 Use a square of white card/cardboard as thick as a cereal box, about 5cm (2in) square. You will also need a pen or pencil.

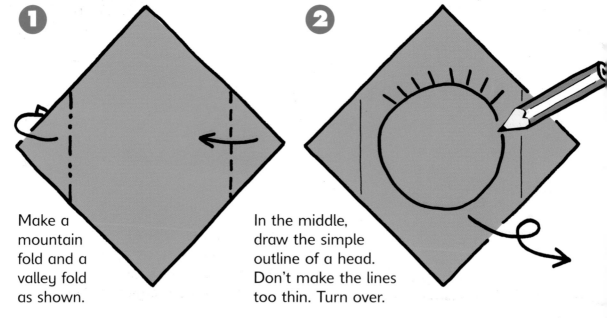

1

Make a mountain fold and a valley fold as shown.

2

In the middle, draw the simple outline of a head. Don't make the lines too thin. Turn over.

3 On the back, draw eyes and a mouth inside where you think the circle would be on the other side.

Tip: Place the card against a bright window to see through the card. Again, don't make the lines too thin.

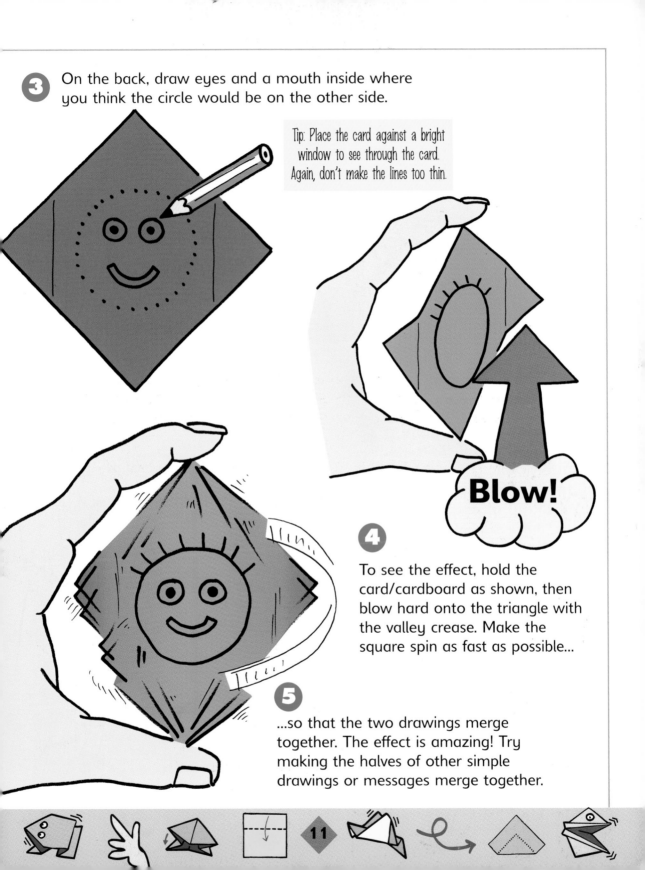

Blow!

4 To see the effect, hold the card/cardboard as shown, then blow hard onto the triangle with the valley crease. Make the square spin as fast as possible...

5 ...so that the two drawings merge together. The effect is amazing! Try making the halves of other simple drawings or messages merge together.

Waterbomb

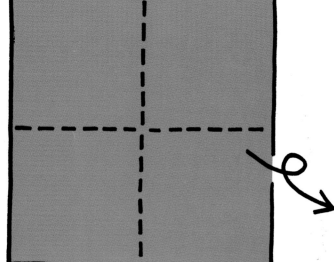

Here's one of the greatest of all origami designs—an all-time true classic. The secret is to learn how to lock it at Step 11 so that it doesn't explode when inflated. Follow the instructions carefully.

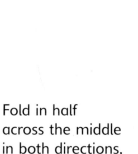
Use a 15–20cm (6–8in) square of paper.

1

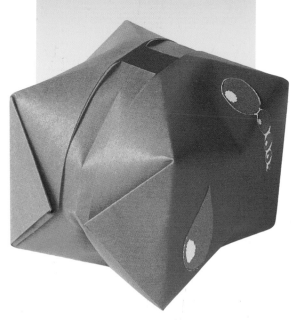

Fold in half across the middle in both directions, then unfold.

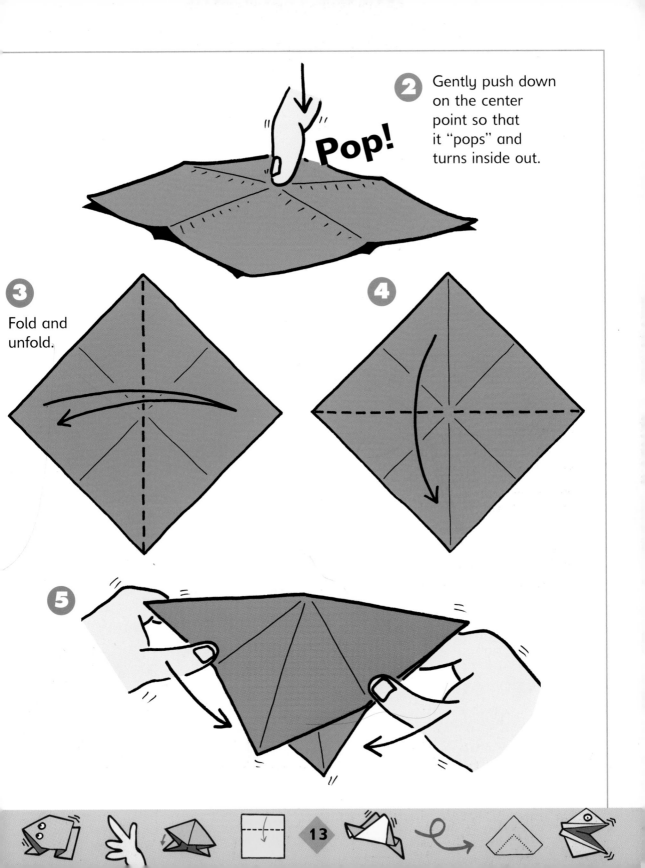

Pop!

2 Gently push down on the center point so that it "pops" and turns inside out.

3 Fold and unfold.

4

5

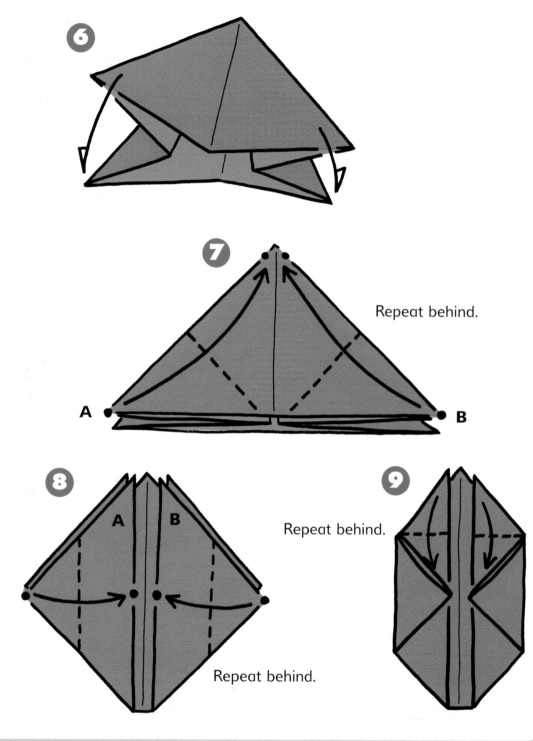

6

7

Repeat behind.

A   B

8

A   B

Repeat behind.

Repeat behind.

9

Repeat behind.

10

Fold and unfold. Repeat behind.

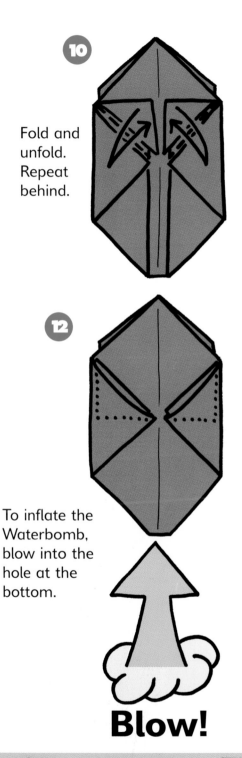

11

This is the important lock. Using the creases made in Step 10, tuck the small triangles deep into the pockets (between the layers) of the larger triangles. It can sometimes be hard to find these pockets, so look very carefully at the drawing to see where they are. Repeat behind.

12

To inflate the Waterbomb, blow into the hole at the bottom.

Blow!

13

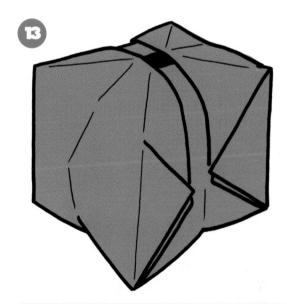

Tip: By keeping A and B separate in Steps 7–8, the hole is made large enough to blow into and so the Waterbomb is easy to inflate. If A and B touch in Step 8, the hole is too small for the Waterbomb to inflate. Also, a larger hole means that it is easy to fill with water!

Jumping Frog

With practice, this athletic favorite will perform a 2m (6ft) long jump or 60cm (2ft) high jump.

For best results, use a small 8 x 5cm (3½ x 2in) rectangle of stiff paper or card cut from a cereal box. You might like to practice with a bigger piece first.

1

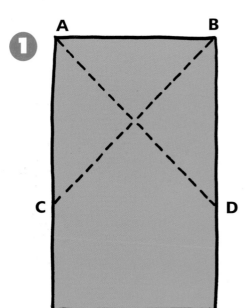

A   B

C   D

2

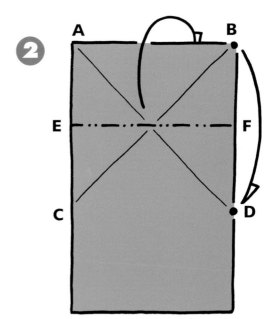

A   B

E   F

C   D

3 Push down on the center point where all the creases meet, so that the card "pops" gently inside out!

Pop!

E

C

A

F

B

D

4 Collapse all the creases ...

A

C

E

F

B

D

5 ... like this. Watch how all the lettered corners move.

A
C

B
D

E F

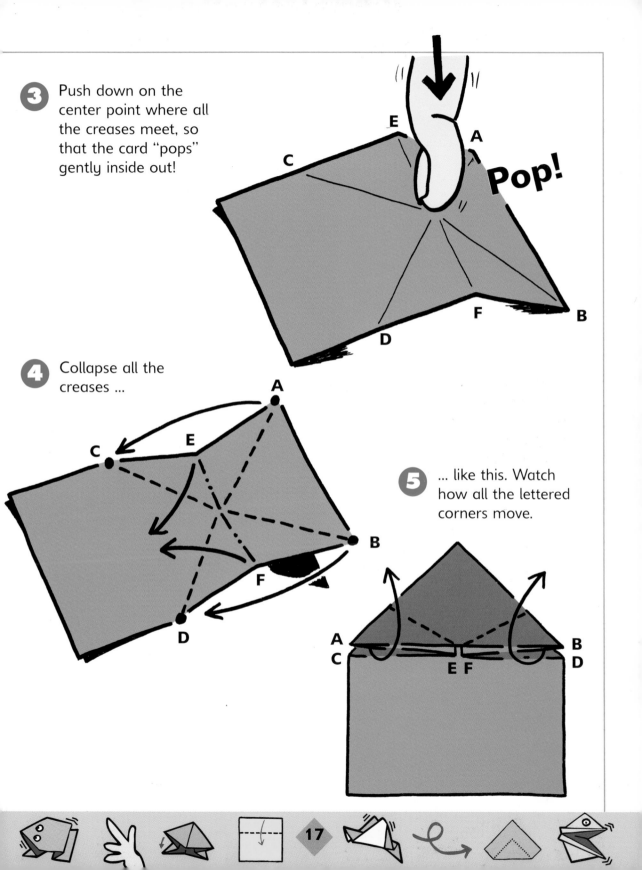

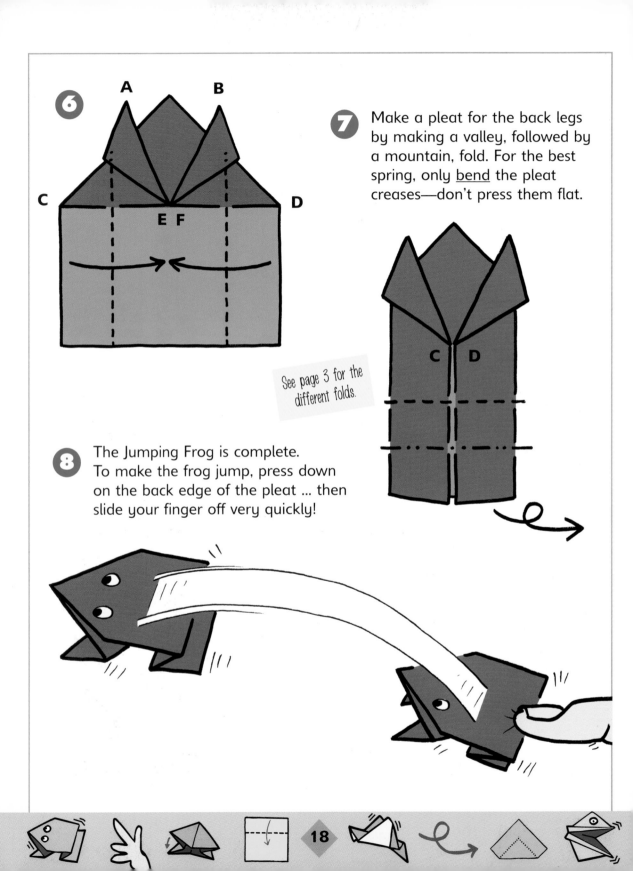

6

A   B

C   D

E F

7 Make a pleat for the back legs by making a valley, followed by a mountain, fold. For the best spring, only <u>bend</u> the pleat creases—don't press them flat.

See page 3 for the different folds.

C   D

8 The Jumping Frog is complete. To make the frog jump, press down on the back edge of the pleat ... then slide your finger off very quickly!

Jaws

These loud and powerful jaws make excellent puppets when eyes and teeth are drawn on.

 Use a 15–20cm (6–8in) square of paper, perhaps a little smaller if your hands are small. You will also need a pair of scissors and some colored felt-tip pens.

1 Fold in half across the middle in both directions, then unfold. Then fold as shown.

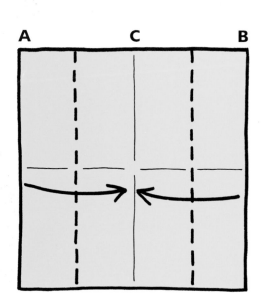

2

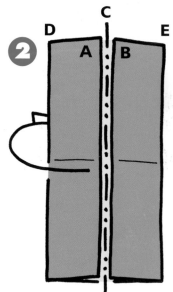

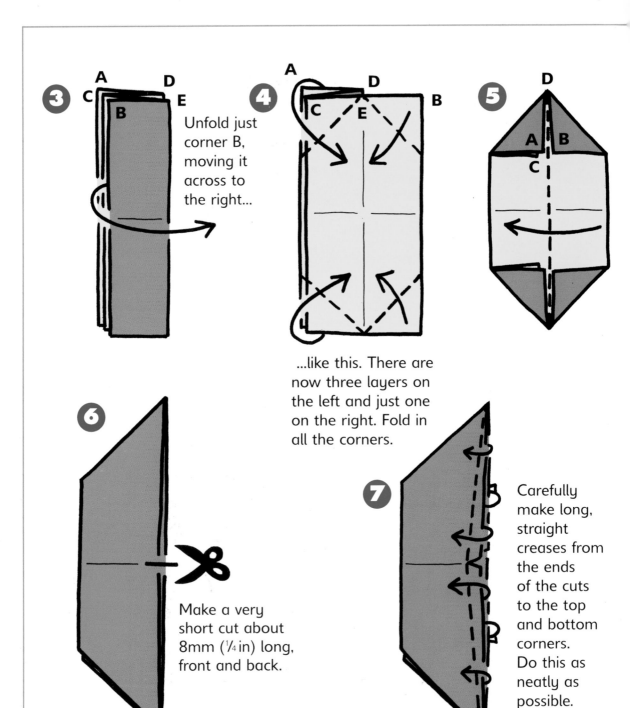

3 **A** **D**
C **E**
B

Unfold just corner B, moving it across to the right...

4 **A** **D** **B**
C **E**

...like this. There are now three layers on the left and just one on the right. Fold in all the corners.

5 **D**
A **B**
C

6

Make a very short cut about 8mm (¼ in) long, front and back.

7

Carefully make long, straight creases from the ends of the cuts to the top and bottom corners. Do this as neatly as possible.

8 To make the Jaws work, hold as shown ... then "Snap!" the jaws quickly together.

9

With colored felt-tip pens, add eyes and teeth, perhaps even a tongue inside the mouth.

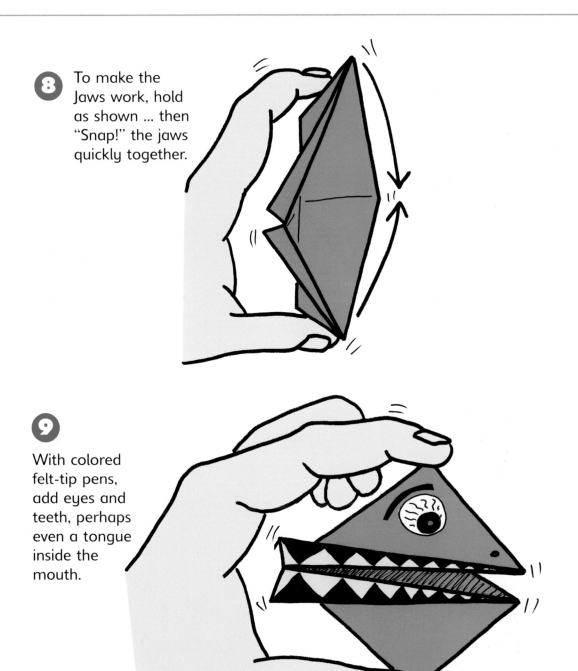

Propeller

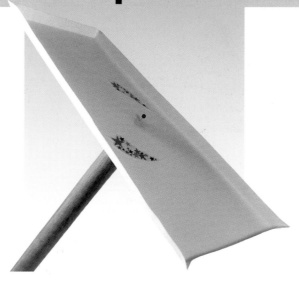

**Not many action origami toys can be made as big as this propeller.
What is the largest one that you can make?
Can you make tiny ones that work, too?**

 Use a rectangle of drawing paper, twice as long as it is high, around 40 x 20cm (16 x 8in). You will also need a pushpin or thumbtack, and a broom with a wooden handle.

1

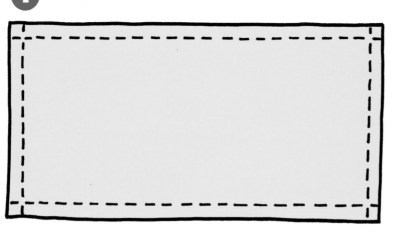

2

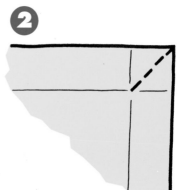

Make the creases no more than 2cm
(¾ in) from the edge.

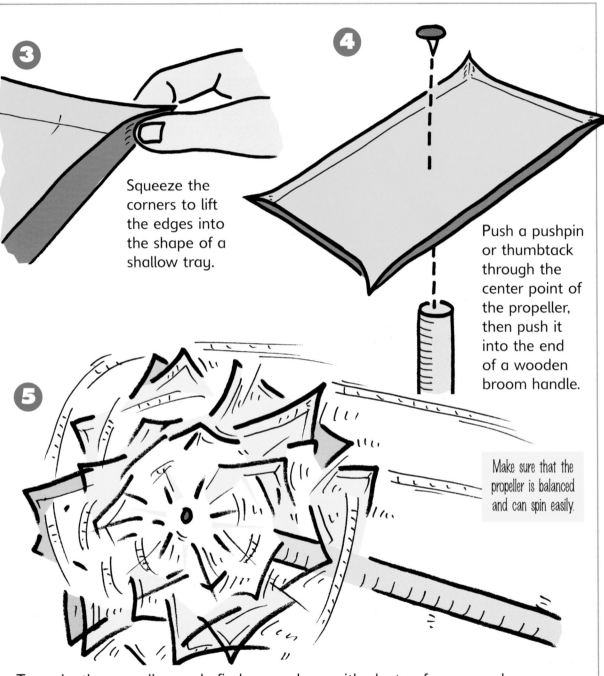

3 Squeeze the corners to lift the edges into the shape of a shallow tray.

4 Push a pushpin or thumbtack through the center point of the propeller, then push it into the end of a wooden broom handle.

5 Make sure that the propeller is balanced and can spin easily.

To make the propeller work, find somewhere with plenty of space, perhaps outside. Hold the brush end of the broom handle, so that the propeller end points straight ahead. Then walk or run forward ... and the propeller will begin to spin! The faster you move, the faster it will spin.

Whip-Crack

The two long, thick strips of paper made here are slapped together at such an incredible speed, they make an amazingly loud "Crack!" sound.

Use 21.5 x 28cm (8½ x 11in) paper and tape.

1 Fold in half across the middle in both directions and unfold. Then fold one side into the middle and unfold.

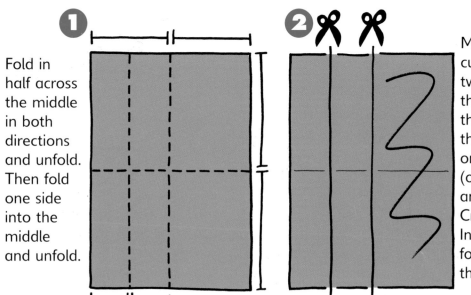

2 Make two long cuts. Keep the two strips on the left, but throw away the large piece on the right (or make another Whip-Crack with it). In Steps 3–5, fold both strips the same way.

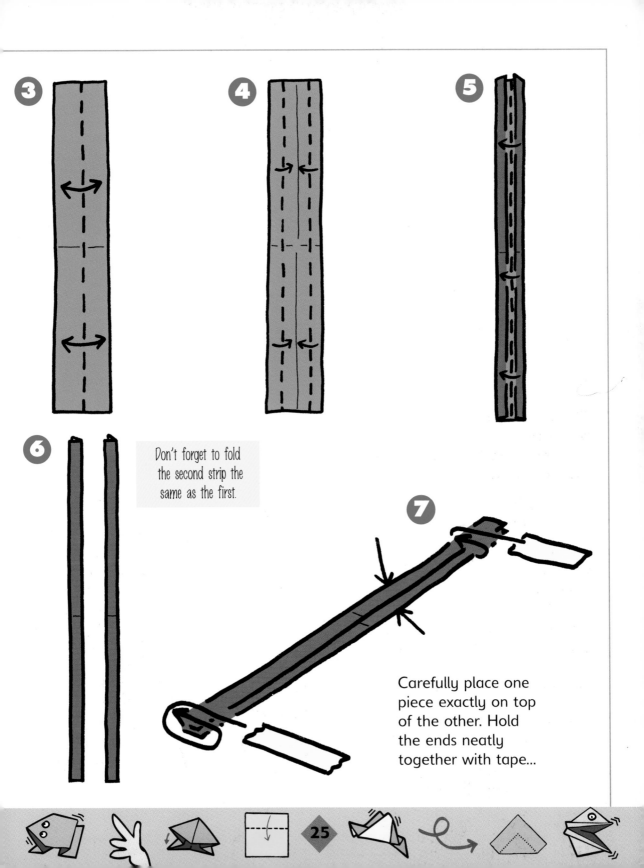

3

4

5

6

Don't forget to fold
the second strip the
same as the first.

7

Carefully place one
piece exactly on top
of the other. Hold
the ends neatly
together with tape...

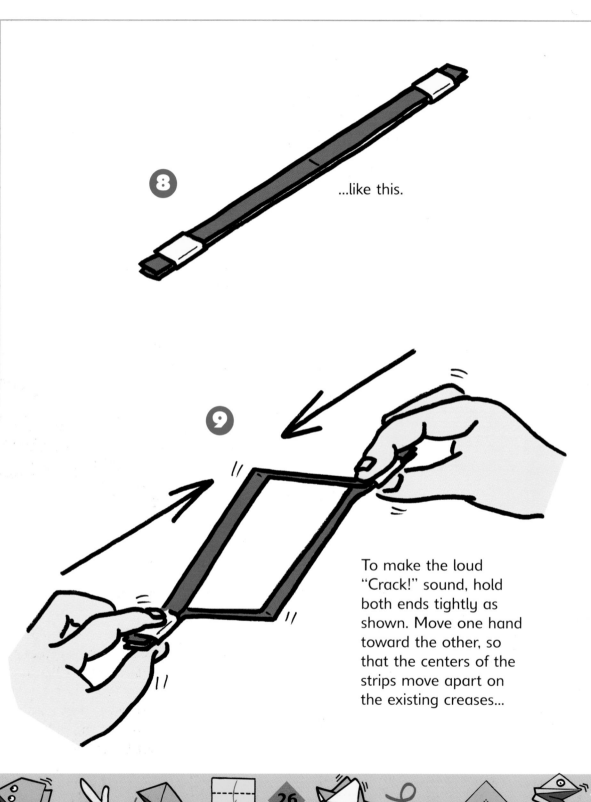

8 ...like this.

9

To make the loud "Crack!" sound, hold both ends tightly as shown. Move one hand toward the other, so that the centers of the strips move apart on the existing creases...

10

...like this. Then as fast as you possibly can, pull your hand quickly away again...

11

CRACK!

...so that the two pieces slap together with a loud "CRACK!" Your hand may be moving so fast that it slides off the paper, but that's OK!

Flapping Bird

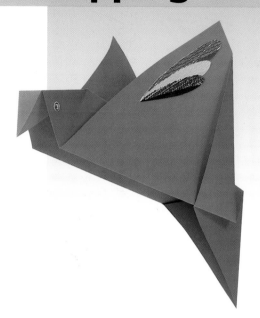

Of all the designs in the book, this is the most difficult. So, be sure to look with special care at the drawings, and read all the instructions. It is certainly a challenge, but it is also the design that will most impress your friends when you show it to them.

1

Use a 15–20cm (6–8in) square of paper.

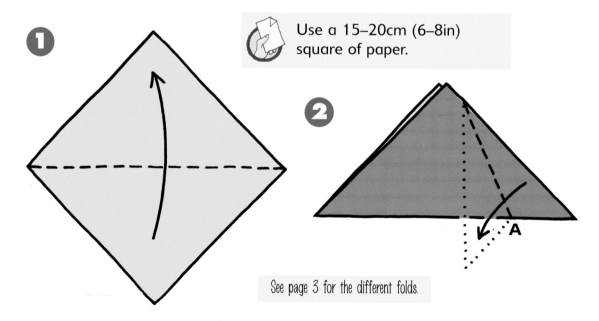

2

See page 3 for the different folds.

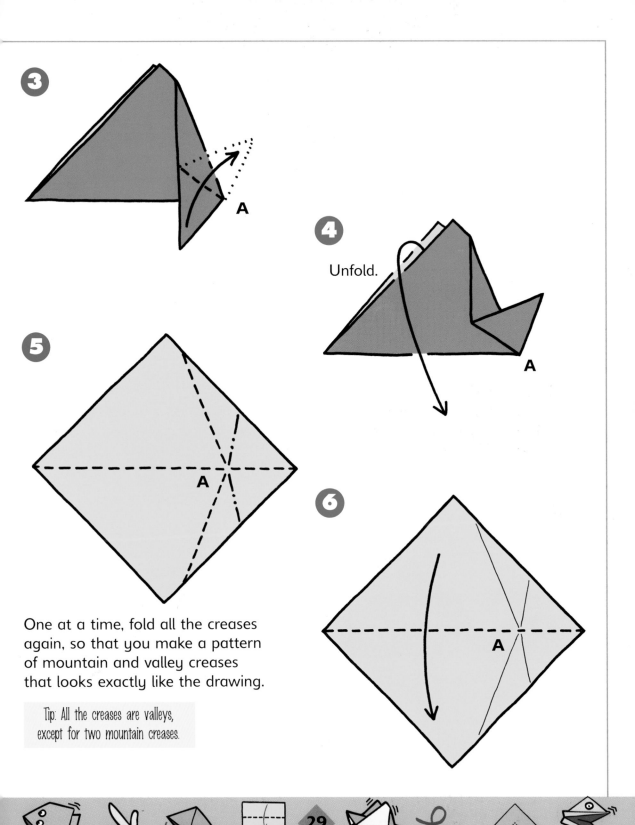

3

A

4

Unfold.

A

5

A

One at a time, fold all the creases again, so that you make a pattern of mountain and valley creases that looks exactly like the drawing.

Tip: All the creases are valleys, except for two mountain creases.

6

A

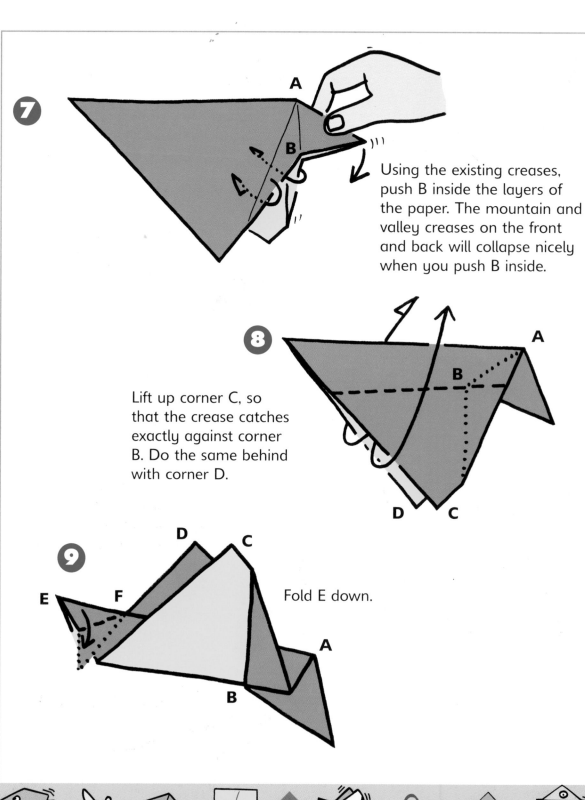

7 Using the existing creases, push B inside the layers of the paper. The mountain and valley creases on the front and back will collapse nicely when you push B inside.

8 Lift up corner C, so that the crease catches exactly against corner B. Do the same behind with corner D.

9 Fold E down.

10

Unfold corner E a little. Make two mountain folds to F and a valley between E and F. Then, collapse all the creases at the same time, to make ...

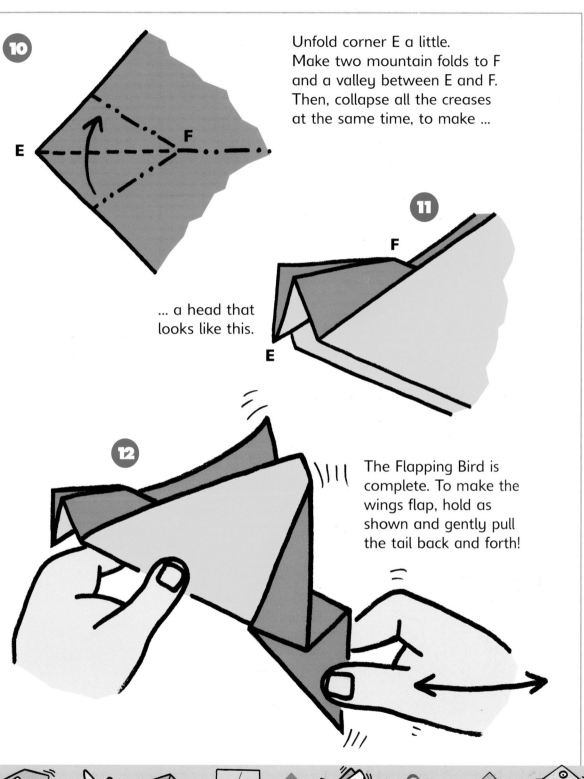

E

F

11

F

... a head that looks like this.

E

12

The Flapping Bird is complete. To make the wings flap, hold as shown and gently pull the tail back and forth!

First published in Great Britain in 2000 by
MARY FORD BOOKS
a division of Michael O'Mara Holdings,
9 Lion Yard, Tremadoc Road, London SW4 7NQ

American edition published by Lowell House
A division of NTC/Contemporary Publishing Group, Inc.
4255 West Touhy Avenue, Lincolnwood (Chicago), Illinois 60712 U.S.A.

Design: Leishman Design
Photography: Meg Sullivan Photography

Lowell House books can be purchased at special discounts
when ordered in bulk for premiums and special sales.
Contact Customer Service at the U.S. address above,
or call 1–800–323–4900.

Printed and made in China.

ISBN 0-7373-0516-9

10 9 8 7 6 5 4 3 2 1